16810

	DATE DUE		

Bright Harbor

Bright Harbor

BY

DANIEL WHITEHEAD HICKY

NEW YORK

HENRY HOLT AND COMPANY

First Printing

PRINTED IN THE UNITED STATES OF AMERICA

BY QUINN & BODEN COMPANY, INC., RAHWAY, N. J.

Acknowledgment

The author thanks the editors of the following magazines and periodicals for their kind permission to reprint the poems in this book:

THE FORUM

THE CARILLON

THE YALE REVIEW

HARPER'S MAGAZINE

HOLLANDS MAGAZINE

SCRIBNER'S MAGAZINE

THE NEW YORK TIMES

THE SATURDAY EVENING POST

POETRY—A MAGAZINE OF VERSE

THE POETRY SOCIETY OF GEORGIA

HERALD TRIBUNE SUNDAY MAGAZINE

THE NORTH AMERICAN REVIEW

THE GRAND MAGAZINE, LONDON

THE GOLDEN BOOK MAGAZINE

WOMAN AND HOME, LONDON

THE LADIES' HOME JOURNAL

THE NEW YORK AMERICAN

THE NEW YORK SUN

THE CATHOLIC WORLD

MCCALL'S MAGAZINE

GOOD HOUSEKEEPING

THE COMMONWEAL

HARPER'S BAZAAR

THE LYRIC

Contents

Bright Harbor

The Victors

They shall come on their day, the humble ones,
The sparrow and the linnet and the lark,
Claiming their own bright moons, their whirling suns,
Their forests sanctuaried in the dark.
They shall burst open their little throats in song,
Nor know a hand, a footfall nor a shell
To cease their singing high and shrill and strong,
But chiming each to each like a great bell,
Their songs will shake the forests, shatter the leaves
Turning from summer to the autumn's gold;
There shall not be one feathered heart that grieves,
Dragging a broken wing it cannot fold.
They shall come on their day. Their day will dawn
When down the roads of Time all men are gone.

The squirrel and the rabbit whose soft feet
Fall light as snowflakes in the drifting snow,
The emerald lizard and the wild and fleet
Young field-mouse and the chipmunk—they shall know
No sharp bewilderment to light their eyes
Seeking for quarry when the fireflies burn
Like yellow jasmine where the daylight dies,
Waking the crickets in the darkening fern.
With all the joy of morning they shall find
A new world where the dew is newly laid,
And drowse in scented grasses where the wind
Strikes harmonies on every quivering blade.

The fields shall lift for them their fairest flower,
Crimson burning on crimson, hour by hour.

They shall come on their day, the fish that swim
The shining waters lightly as a dream,
Knowing no line to snatch them, knowing no dim
Half-hidden hook set in a sunlit stream.
They shall swim onward where the waters flow
Beneath the shadows of the willow trees,
Carving their lyric rhythms, swift and slow,
Leaping and falling with their silver ease.
Blue hyacinths shall open wide and spread
Their petals on the waters like a fan,
Knowing no mortal hand that long has bled
Them of their blossoms. (Beauty-starving man!)
They shall come on their day, the fish that ply
Beneath the hyacinths under a watching sky.

And little men shall sleep, lover to lover,
Victorious and the vanquished, each to each,
Nor hear the feet of humble ones go over
The dust of them, the dust of all their speech,
The dust of all their motors laid aside,
One with the earth again, one with the earth.
They shall come from the forests in all their pride,
Claiming new stars that leap from fiery birth,
Claiming the roads that man could never share,
Claiming the mountains where their songs can flow,
The lanes of laurel harboring no snare.
Over the earth, triumphant, they shall go
Stirring the dust where little men are laid—
The furred and feathered, eager, unafraid.

Always, Always

Always, always, it will be thus: the sun
Unfolded like a blinding marigold,
The bright noon's fiery embers swiftly done
And twilight scattering shadows blue and cold.
April upon the bough and all too brief,
The ripened fruit, and leaves that bleed and burn,
Young lovers with their passions and their grief,
Age hoarding dreams like petals in an urn.
Always, always, it has been thus since Time
Unloosed the emerald rhythms of the sea,
Since first the white-winged moon began to climb
The purple night. Beloved, and what are we
But less than the dark quiver of a flower,
We with our little words, our little hour?

Harbor Song

Now I am never one to say
    I do not love her lips
As scarlet as camellias are;
    Her petaled finger tips
Like oleanders underneath
    A yellow Southern moon,
And all the things she says to me
    And every lilting tune.
But somehow, I forget her eyes,
    Hydrangea-blue, her lips,
When I go down along the harbor
    Watching all the ships.

For I am lost in watching gulls
    Circle back and forth
In shining rhythms with the ships
    Sailing South, sailing North;
And shouts of sweating stevedores
    Are music to my ear
Loading grapes and golden fruit
    And singing high and clear;
And every sail tugs at my heart
    And every ship says "Come!—
Barcelona, Timbuktu,
    Valencia, Byzantium!"

My love can never understand
    At night beside the fire

Why my thoughts are wander-like
  As flames leap higher and higher.
It does not mean I love her less,
  (O breasts like pale moonflowers,
O haunting songs she sings to me
  Through all the dark's blue hours!)
But somehow, I forget my love,
  Her eyes, her songs, her lips,
When I go down along the harbor
  Watching all the ships.

A Ship for Singapore

A ship is sailing for Singapore!
O heart be swift and latch the door!

My fire burns bright and the shadows fall
In yellow rhythms along the wall.
My love sleeps near and her dreams are deep,
Her lips a rose that has fallen asleep.
The fire burns bright and the candles glow,
And I must not go—I must not go!

There is no peace I can know to-night
Though my love sleeps near and the fire burns bright,
For stars will call from an Indian sky
And a gold moon haunt me blowing by.
The sea's wild horses will leap and fly,
Foam on their manes and wind in their eye!

O heart be swift and latch the door—
A ship is sailing for Singapore!

Inscription for a Sundial

Senseless with beauty pressing like a flame
Around me in this sunlit garden-close—
Blue of the larkspur, yellow of the rose,
White lilies holier than any name—
What can I be that I have earned a place
Where tulips ring their gold cathedral bell,
Where poppies lean upon the air and tell
Their scarlet secrets with an upturned face?
What right have I to know the touch of things
Intangible as wind and shadows' wings,
Things that can never know there is an hour,
A day, a year, only eternity;
Oh, what am I to stand here patiently
And count away the heartbeats of a flower?

They Know When Aprils Come

They know when Aprils come—the dear dead lovers
Of yesteryear who sleep so quietly
Beneath the silence of the snow's white covers
That lay them under, softly, tenderly.
They know when waking passion stirs a seed
And dark roots throb with rhythms they have lost;
When hills are alive with colors that burn and bleed—
Blooms only the spendthrift Beauty could have tossed.
No April takes the meadows past their knowing,
No rose goes out in scarlet but they hear
Its petals in a wave of wildfire blowing
Along the emerald highways of the year.
No Aprils come, but restless as a wing
The dust of lovers stirs, remembering.

Full Moon

Since we are not the first we shall not be
The last of lovers seeking this dark lane
Where lilacs stir like promises of rain
Among the quiet leaves. Eternity
Shall find them here, each with their eager lips
Building a dream from lovers' tenderness,
Shaping a shining world from loveliness—
A world that crumbles at their finger tips.
If we return a thousand years away
We shall come on this lane; it will be here
With lilacs' breath grown deeper and lovelier,
And we shall find them with young eyes alight
Saying the old words over that now we say,
With stars still grazing on the slopes of night.

To a Youth Killed in Battle

You did not merely give your last heartbeat;
You gave your heritage of seas and ships,
Your birthright of long roads and gypsy feet,
Of starlit hilltops and of lovers' lips.
The silver of a thousand moons you tossed,
A gay young spendthrift on the fields of death,
Nor for one moment did you count the cost—
The crimson flare, the last sweet spark of breath!
You gave far more, far more than that last drop
Of blood that sang its passion through your veins;
Your glorious sacrifice shall never stop
Though you are dust beneath the Flanders rains.
For Age can give one life when life is done,
But youth, ah, youth!—a thousand lives in one!

When Each White Cloud

When each white cloud has reached its destination
Across the cool blue oceans of the sky,
And every rose's crimson conflagration
Of beauty burns to ashes, I shall lie
One with the insignificant dust, nor know
In that dark silence how the slow dawns broke
In ripening fires across impatient hills,
Nor how at dusk the ivory moonflowers woke
To claim their little hour. Time will flow
Above me like a wind that stirs and stills
The dust, to still and stir the dust again;
I shall forget all earth, its babbling men,
Remembering only where the dark is deep
That you and I have loved; then I shall sleep.

Deep South

The cotton ripens best on nights like this:
  A hot night with a yellow moon that goes
Above the huddled cabins, touching them
    Almost, and swinging past the farthest rows.

Above the bayous where the willows lean
    Tremulous with silence, heavy with the dark,
A hundred fireflies light and light again
    Rippling the stagnant waters with their spark.

And black young lovers sweating in their slumber
    Turn to each other under the moon's warm light
Forgetting the stretching fields, with honeysuckle
    Deep as an arrow in the heart of night.

Say That He Loved Old Ships

Say that he loved old ships; write nothing more
Upon the stone above his resting place;
And they who read will know he loved the roar
Of breakers white as starlight, shadow lace
Of purple twilights on a quiet sea,
First ridge of daybreaks in a waiting sky,
The wings of gulls that beat eternally
And haunt old harbors with their silver cry.
Speak softly now, his heart has earned its rest,
This heart that knew each alien star by name,
Knew passion of the waves against his breast
When clouds swept down the sea and lightning's flame
Tore skies asunder with swift finger tips;
Write nothing more; say that he loved old ships.

Snowstorm

All through the night I could not sleep for waking
At every pleading of the wind's distress,
And hearing cedars breaking, breaking, breaking,
Heaped with too much of crystal loveliness.
Along the lane they knelt like nuns in prayer,
Like rosaries they told the hours of night;
And still the snow's white petals thundered there
Like dust of meteors quivering and white.
How could I sleep with so much beauty falling,
A rain of stars upon the frozen ground,
The night wind hungry as a wolf, and calling
For shelter that is sought but never found—
I who have seen how snowflakes break apart
The cedar boughs, as beauty breaks the heart?

We with Our Vanities

We with our vanities and bright opinions,
  Our swiftly flashing tongue and quickening eye,
I wonder if we know that we are lesser
  Than any shadow we are measured by?

We polish up dull words until they glitter,
  Sharpen our wits like knives and shape our creed,
Yet who amongst us does not cringe, half-frightened,
  Hearing a slow breath stirring in a seed?

Wrapped in deep solitudes we fashion motors
  Shattering the silence, musical with power,
And yet—where is the wheel that turns, unfolding
  A single rose before its scarlet hour?

Requiem for a Young Poet

They pause beside your grave, and, pitying, pass
Lightly as wind along the grass.
"Ah, life's bright coins unspent, its songs unsung!"
They say of you who died so young.

They have not seen you take the road at dawn
With sunrise in your face, the wind upon
Your eager shoulders like a shining cloak,
Marsh lilies' incense drifting thin as smoke
Along the hot road where cool shadows were laid
In patterns like a green brocade.
They have not seen you wade knee-deep
In tides of asters pale as sleep,
Nor in the sunset followed where
You drank its gold wine, cold and clear.

They cannot know how in the dusk you came,
Calling each slumbering flower by name,
Seeing them waking, shaking the dew,
Speaking their fragile words to you.
They have not seen you go when evening fell
Softly as music of an unrung bell,
Into the darkness singing a poet's tune,
Filling your eyes with the light of the moon,
Counting the stars and watching them dim
As day came over the night's blue rim.

They weep for you, and, pitying, pass
Lightly as wind along the grass.
"Ah, life's bright coins unspent, its songs unsung!"
They say of you who died so young.

Machines

I hear them grinding, grinding, through the night,
The gaunt machines with arteries of fire,
Muscled with iron, boweled with smoldering light;
I watch them pulsing, swinging, climbing higher,
Derrick on derrick, wheel on rhythmic wheel,
Swift band on whirring band, lever on lever,
Shouting their songs in raucous notes of steel,
Blinding a village with light, damming a river.
I hear them grinding, grinding, hour on hour,
Cleaving the night in twain, shattering the dark
With all the rasping torrents of their power,
Groaning and belching spark on crimson spark.
I cannot hear my voice above their cry
Shaking the earth and thundering to the sky.

Slowly the dawn comes up. No motors stir
The brightening hilltops as the sunrise flows
In yellow tides where daybreak's lavender
Clings to a waiting valley. No derrick throws
The sun into the heavens and no pulley
Unfolds the wildflowers thirsting for the day;
No wheel unravels ferns deep in a gulley;
No engine starts the brook upon its way.
The butterflies drift idly, wing to wing,
Knowing no measured rhythm they must follow;
No turbine drives the white clouds as they swing
Across the cool blue meadows of the swallow.
With all the feathered silence of a swan
They whirr and beat—the engines of the dawn.

The Watchers

Let us be silent for a little space,
Watching the slow stars brighten one by one;
There will be time for words when stars are done.
Upon this hillside tangled with shadow lace
What are we lovers in the scheme of things?
Above us sweep the Pleiades; Aldebaran
Whirls in a yellow flame, and Venus swings
Brighter than any dream of any man;
Arcturus burns upon its charted way,
Orion flares nor slows its fiery pace.
Worlds float above us. Beneath this hill of clay
Pulse seas we shall not know in our brief day.
Turn to me now your dear, bewildered face;
Let us be silent for a little space.

April Takes a Battlefield

How silently April takes a battlefield!
There is no flare of trumpets and no drum,
No flash of armor and no glittering shield
To mark the sudden way that she will come.
There is no blood upon the winter's breast,
No bayonet sunk deep within his heart,
No cry of anguish rising, crest on crest,
To shake the valleys and the hills apart.
But softly as the falling of the rain,
Unheralded as the opening of a flower,
The dawn will find her legions on each plain,
Victorious, defiant, her bright hour.
And though the armies of the earth shall beat
Upon her stronghold, they will know defeat.

The Hunters

Their shot had wrung the wild duck from the sky
And they had shouted as its flight was broken
To see it plunge to swift eternity;
Victorious now they stood, with no word spoken.
Bleeding, it lay upon the cool marsh grass
Quivering with agony of its last flight;
Jesting, they watched the last faint flutter pass
Less than a shadow in the falling night.
Lightly they pushed their boat across the lake,
The weeping of their oar the only stir
As darkness rippled in the dark boat's wake
And gathered up the day's last lavender.
They broke in laughter and began to sing
But I could hear only a folded wing.

Sonnets of Nightfall

Always I shall remember how the night
Comes on a garden. There can never be
A silence deeper than the day's last light
Brings to a closing petal. Sleepily,
A tulip yawns and nods upon the wind,
A bluebell tinkles faintly; four o'clocks
Forget that Time beats on eternally,
Folded in crimson slumber. Hollyhocks
Breathe delicately as music that is thinned
To memory; a bee sways on the stocks
Where shadows hide his golden piracy.
The moon comes slowly, and its white hand rocks
The gate until the last bright firefly goes
Into the dark cathedral of a rose.

This is the hour for lovers. Close the door
And turn the latch, ye old and weary-eyed;
The white moon climbs the sky for you no more.
This is youth's hour. These bright stars, tide on tide,
Swirling from purple anvils of the night
Are but for lovers' hearts. The dark wind sings
Only for lips that meet when moons are white,
Only for hearts that know no perishings.
Let them gather shadows about them and go
Light-hearted, where lilacs hang heavy and still
With the new-fallen dew; let them whisper low,
Forgetting that dawn waits over the hill.
It is the hour for lovers when shadows creep;
Ye old and weary, close the door, and sleep.

Seashore

The sun rides on the water like a ship
Masted with flame. Far out, two seagulls dip

And meet again, white breast to swerving breast,
And rise, and soon are lost upon a quest.

The sea is but a stretch of silence now—
Blue silence. Soon a sailing boat's swift prow

Will carve a foam-white pathway and be gone,
A shining memory to linger on.

I watch the clouds. Slowly they drift away,
As white as any prayer a nun could pray.

I trace my name into the brightening beach
And laugh, for soon the fingering tide will reach

Inward and bear it outward to be tossed
Like topaz dust that glitters and is lost.

I try to sleep. My ears are each a shell
That holds the sea's slow music, swell on swell.

This is a day without an end. I know
No hour that I may rise and turn and go,

Leaving the bright waves running, hand in hand,
Their silver marathons along the sand.

· 25 ·

The Bargainers

The Summer asked of Autumn yesterday:
"What will you give me for these fading flowers,
These twilights that I bring; these darkening hours
Throbbing with perfume still? What will you pay?"
And Autumn pondered, fingering the things
That Summer brought: a scarlet rose, half-bled,
A bough of honeysuckle and a red
And yellow pair of butterfly's bright wings.
And Autumn held them coldly to the light:
"This flower shatters on my finger tips;
This butterfly is far too tired to fly;
I offer you but lodging for the night."
And Summer wept. All songs died on her lips,
Taking the road when dawn burned in the sky.

Marsh Twilight

The lake has drawn the last gold from the sun
And holds it like a mirror to the sky;
Marsh grasses tremble slowly, one by one,
As if a wing and not the wind goes by.
The finger tips of purple shadows creep
In quiet rhythms down the darkening lake,
And dusk grows deep with color, like a sleep
Too haunted with its dreaming to awake.
A lone white heron stirs to sudden flight
And all is shadow once again, and gold
That fringes still the garment of the night.
Now crickets break the silence that is rolled
Away as swiftly as the twilight came;
The moon comes up, a bird with wings of flame.

Deep Summer

The fields are ripe with summer. Daisies blow
In silver tides with whitecaps of the sun,
And there is silent music in their flow
Beneath the butterflies whose wings are spun
From dust of all the summers that have been.
The brook is dry and tangled with brown fern;
The moss's slow processional of green
Across a stone, a bud that soon will burn
Into a blackberry flower, are all that Spring
Bequeaths to-day. The torrid sun slips low;
The West is suddenly afire. I fling
My book aside, and with a cry, I throw
Myself into the daisies that shall soon
Be beating their white breakers on the moon.

Sunrise

Beloved, how sweet this light upon the pane
Bringing the sunrise to the waiting world,
Clearing the fields of nightfall, opening again
The morning glories that the darkness furled.
How good to hear magnolia branches shaking
With early sparrows, and below our sill
The brook grown musical as though awaking
From some deep dream that held it strangely still.
Seeing the dark room flood with drifting light,
And you beside me through this miracle
Wrought from the utter blackness of the night,
How sweet to hear you, beautiful with sleep,
Breathing in rhythms like a slow-rung bell,
Dawn giving back all that my heart would keep.

Sailors' Women

Blue with the dusk I watch them gathering
Along the edges of the sea-port town,
Old women with twisted canes, young girls that sing,
Sweet-scented harlots in their brightest gown.
I hear their chatter like a nest of sparrows,
Their high-pitched laughter and the slow guitars,
Watching them treading down the cobbled narrows
To pier-ends where the lanterns swing like stars.
A light drifts over the harbor and a sail
Purple with darkness, hides the moon away;
Slowly it drifts and slowly the light grows pale;
Suddenly a path of fire lights up the bay.
This is the hour when all their grief is over
And the sea gives back to the heart its lover.

Like crystal are the names come home again:
Josef, and Halvar, Michelangelo,
Christus whose eyes still hold the sun of Spain;—
With sea-wet lips now arm in arm they go
Swinging their women up the darkened hill,
Tasting of pudding ere they reach the door,
Seeing the candles lighted at their sill,
Knowing that firelight dances on the floor.
Soon they will lie abed with breasts as white
As lotus flowers opening in the dark,
Their lips be crushed with kisses through the night,
Their veins pulse with slow music till a spark

Of smoldering daybreak drifts across the skies
Lighting the panes of their brief paradise.

Down to the wharves again the women will come—
Rosa, Carlotta, Ingrid, laughing, weeping,
Begging for silks and pearls and jugs of rum,
Giving their lovers to the sea's dark keeping.
Slowly the ship will sail, slowly the sun
Turn every sail to fires of sudden gold,
And with the full moon's rising once begun,
Be lost beyond horizons far and cold.
Only the women of sailors can know
Their love is shared; only the women of sailors
Believe through the day and the night it is so—
Fast at the wheels of the clippers and whalers.
Thus do they weep when they meet and they part,
Knowing the sea shares the love of their heart.

This Is the End

This is the end. Let now no quickened word
Break silence of our lips grown suddenly wise,
But turn and go like shadows that are stirred
To silent flight when sunrise takes the skies.
Nor come again. One cannot mend a flower
Shaken to shattered petals in the night;
The candles will burn out another hour,
So turn and go while yet there is a light.
Nor seek to put together what is gone—
No broken song can be a song again;
Best to remember as time passes on,
The last deep note of any song's refrain;
Best to forget my eyes, my lips, my name . . .
A candle is no light without a flame.

To a Garden Snail

Making no sound but silence as you pass
Tracing a silver highway through the grass,

Stirring no leaf nor twig upon your way
Beneath the closing shadows of the day,

Unheralded, alone, and quite alone,
I watch you seek a cool, moss-conquered stone.

Seeing you slowly pass before my feet
Crushing the grasses heavy with dew, and sweet,

I pause, and suddenly I know that I
Have seen God pass in silver and a cry

Wells in my throat. Within your lowly shell
Pulses the heartbeat of the miracle

That fashioned mountains, stretched the farthest wave,
Unfolded flowers on a bare stem, gave

April and autumn to the waiting trees,
Breathed sparks of fire into the Pleiades.

O humble brother, as I pause alone
Watching you seek the shelter of your stone,

Smaller than any grasses you have trod,
Bewildered, I have seen the power of God

Beat in your shell, and He has spoken to me
As surely as in the sun, the stars, the sea.

A Sailor to His Bride

How can my heart be now content to know
A low-thatched roof and springtime at the gate,
A crimson hearthfire and the mellow glow
Of yellow candles when the night grows late?
I who have known the gulls above my head,
The moonlit spray of breakers on my lips—
How can these tender words your heart has said
Be anchorage for me, long loving ships?
Your hands will keep the cups and saucers bright,
And you will sing a song for me each day,
But should you wake one cold and starswept night
And reach for me and I have gone away—
O say a prayer to God with a lifted hand
And ask of Him to help you understand!

Sonnet

When you and I have grown too old for loving
The first slow tide of dawn across the dark,
Too old to pause, bewildered, when a lark
Plunges its arrow of music where we are roving;
When the first rose of April fails to quicken
Our pulse and hold us speechless for a spell,
And we are tired, too tired, to sit and tell
Love's words again, and watch the bright stars
    thicken,—
When comes that hour and the spirit sighs,
Though still we talk as one who understands,
Feel summer's sunlight and the winter's knife,
Ah, little do we know that all of life
Will lie upon a bier with folded hands
And silent lips, and pennies on its eyes.

Finale

There is no death like death that lovers know.
 Old men can slip away
 Like shadows at the door of day,
And are contented so.

The young go like a half-unopened flower
 Awaiting sunlight as its petals part,
 But lovers go with an arrow in their heart—
The last word said in love's last hour.

"He Will Come Back"

"He will come back," she said, and let her hair
Fall like a shower of sunlight on her bare
White shoulders pale as moonflowers are. And then
She turned her eyes out to the sea again.

I did not tell her how the sea's cold fingers
  Clutch at a sailor's throat and hold him fast
  As drunken shadows shackled to the mast
Of ships at dusk; nor how a sailor lingers

Along a harbor bright with amber wings,
  And always finds a far port's music sweet,
  Knows other lips and eyes and maidens' feet
Hungry for dancing where a red moon swings.

She blew the candle's golden blossom out
  And gave herself to sleep as breakers came
  Like silver tigers up the shore, a flame
Of music leaping with a lyric shout.

Her lips were soft against her pillow. Blue
With silence, twilight sought her room and drew
The moonlight in, cool flake on shining flake.
"He will come back," she dreamed. Why must she
    wake?

The Last Hour

We are no stronger than the roses are
In that last hour when the hands of Time
Measuring the blood's slow rhythms pause, and chime;
We who are brave and strong, who wear the scar
Of battles that have wrung our wits apart,
We who have breathed as pauper and as king,
Laughing at life and holding each golden thing
More precious than the beating of our heart;
With knowledge like a rudder in the brain,
Only in that last hour are we wise,
Weighing each waning breath with pleading eyes,
Knowing the blood's last battle all in vain.
It will not vary under any star:
We are no stronger than the roses are.

Endings

Always an ending. Shall I never see
Some glory hidden from the slow sure blade
Beneath whose sharpened edge all things are laid,
All beauty and all love? Can there not be
Some rose that blooms beyond its farthest reach,
A sun that will not leave the blue bright day,
A meadow flower that will not shatter away,
Some wave that is not lost upon the beach?
I fill my eyes with dawn; I drink it deep,
And day is lost to dusk, and dusk to night;
I watch the moon; it blinds me, and I weep
To see it waning like a weary light.
O earth, O sky, O sea! Tell me these lies:
Beauty lives always—and love never dies!

April at Château-Thierry

Tread lightly, April, this is hallowed ground;
Tread lightly as your lyric feet can pass,
And sprinkle, with no shadow of a sound,
Bright crocuses along the tender grass.
Let lilacs softly burst in bloom again,
And spread a carpeting of violets
For silver sandals of the quiet rain
That glitters like the flash of bayonets.
Light up the hills with tulips' wind-blown flame
As acolytes would light an altar-stone;
Twine poppies far too lovely for a name
Around the lonely crosses, one by one.
Tread lightly, April, soft and crystal-clear . . .
A generation's April slumbers here.

And Some Bright Morning

And some bright morning if there be no waking,
No waking when the pendulum of Time
Swings darkness into sunrise; if the breaking
And laughter of my heart be swiftly over,
There will be then no pausing in the chime
Of stars that march victorious down the sky,
And life will thunder on, and twilights hover
Above the far horizons; earth and I
Will be akin again. No wild wind flowing
Its silver hair across the evening's breast
Will half remember me, earth's ardent lover;
No breaking dawn with wide eyes, deep and glowing,
Shall lay a golden finger where I rest;
No cloud shall change its course, be ever knowing!

Rendezvous

When dusk has fallen like a ripened plum
Deep in the wood there is a tryst I keep
In shadows where no heaven-eyed trillium
Would dare intrude, nor pale arbutus creep.
There is a language that my heart must seek
To drown man's babbling trivialities,
For I must talk with quiet things that speak
In syllables of emerald silences.
There a maple drips gold leaves like yellow bells
Yet never speaks of one bough that is hers;
Wood-jasmine in a thousand miracles
Unfolds more stars than any twilight stirs.
Yet I would never know lest I should see;
A talk with forest things is good for me.

Wild Geese

In autumn it is good to pause and listen
  Beside your door and hear the wild geese going
In arrows down the sky; to see them glisten
  With blue and amber of the sunset flowing

Wild as a flame across the marsh. Your mouth
  Grows suddenly speechless, beauty blinds your eye,
And if you listen closely toward the South
  You hear your own heart beating down the sky!

To an Aviator

You who have grown so intimate with stars
  And known their silver dripping from your wings,
Swept with the breaking day across the sky,
  Known kinship with each meteor that swings—

You who have touched the rainbow's fragile gold,
  Carved lyric ways through dawn and dusk and rain
And soared to heights our hearts have only dreamed—
  How can you walk earth's common ways again?

Who Pilots Ships

Who pilots ships knows all a heart can know
Of beauty, and his eyes may close in death
And be content. There is no wind to blow
Whiter than foam-white wind and no wind's breath
Sweeter than tropic wind. There is no star
That throbs with cold white fire as North stars do;
No golden moon-path lovelier than the far
Path burning on the sea when dusk is blue.
There is no rain so swift as rain that flies
In bright battalions with a storm begun,
No song that shakes the heart like amber cries
Of gulls with wings turned yellow in the sun.
Who pilots ships when life's last heartbeats stop
Has drained the cup of beauty drop by drop.

White Journey

It is good to walk in the snow alone
With the cedars bending down,
Wrapping yourself in its quiet,
Forgetting the lights of the town.
It is good to feel on your shoulders
The snow as it shatters and spills
Like the dust of the Pleiades on you
Making your way up the hills,
Leaving a path of white silence
Over the way that you go
With a heart that is beating as lightly
As the falling snow.

You will go with the crunching of crystal
Music beneath your feet,
And the wind's cold fingers strumming
The shining strings of the sleet,
And you will not pause to question
The time of the day or night
For the hours will drift like the snowflakes,
And your every thought, turned white,
Will be of the snow and the silence
And the blue light that is stirred
By shadows swaying beneath the flight
Of a startled hare or a bird.

It is good to know on your journey
There is no word you must say,

No promise to keep in the darkness;
To know, as you ponder your way,
You may journey as far as you choose to,
Nor stop at a single house;
Only you and the snow and the silence
Broken by white cedar boughs
Cracking above and below you
As you trample the underbrush down;
It is good to walk in the snow alone,
Forgetting the lights of the town.

Renunciation

When I am done with worldly things that blind me
　Like a swift light that flashes and is gone,
Deep in a forest the long slow years will find me
　Waiting for the twilight, listening for the dawn.

I shall have time to see a fern uncurling
　Its emerald fingers like a child asleep;
To watch gold fireflies, gypsy-hearted, swirling
　In beauty that the night alone may reap.

I shall have time to hear the scarlet sobbing
　Of shattered roses on a frosted bough;
To hear the breath of early autumn throbbing
　In every grass I trample lightly now.

Then shall I know, and let my heart run over
　With secrets that will open like a flower,
And I will lie in deep sweet-scented clover
　And count the shining minutes of each hour.

So Brief a Thing

So brief a thing is beauty, hold it close,
As closely as your heart would hold a wing
That soon is flown again, unraveling
Its splendor down the lyric way it goes.
Drink sunsets deeply; drink their dregs of rose
That linger in the darkening sky. A thing
Of beauty is a glory that will sing
Its way into your soul. Your blood that flows
Will quicken into music in your veins.
Look long upon all beauty that you see—
The lavender of lilacs and a tree
Armored in sudden silver of the rains.
Hold beauty closely; never let it go
Till eyes are blind and lips are pale as snow.

Plantation Night

The last gold footprint of the sun is gone
And solitude that almost breaks the heart
Has captured every darkening field. Upon
A crisp magnolia leaf the sudden dart
Of homing wings in swift and lyric flight
Awakes the silence of the after-glow,
And oleanders, pale as nuns, drift white
And fragrant petals like new-fallen snow.
Blue shadows fall like finger tips of dream
As quietude wrapped in the gathering dark
Comes down the road, and suddenly, a gleam
Of yellow fireflies, spark on golden spark,
Steals lantern-like from willows by the river
As moonlight listens to the shadows quiver.

To a Persian Rug Weaver

These are not merely yellows and pale blues
Your hands have woven with each twisted thread;
Not merely mauve and gold and saffron hues—
They are your hunger for a crust of bread.
This lavender is dreaming you have known,
This turquoise is the laughter you have lost,
This thread that deepens to a silver tone,
Old memory as white as sudden frost.
You did not merely weave a pattern there
Of twisted rainbows from an April sky,
Deep breath of roses on the Persian air,
A desert song in every throbbing dye;
This is no passing symbol of an art—
Here is the very beating of your heart!

Autumn Again

Autumn again, and the old summer going
  In arrows of beauty swift on the wind;
Sycamore, oak, and the maple's leaves blowing,
  Glorious legions that soon shall be thinned!

Southward they fly like a ribbon aflutter,
  Bright with their splendor, the birds with a cry
That cuts at the heart! What mortal could utter
  A word or a song that would shatter the sky?

Autumn again, and the old summer going,
  Deep valleys yellow with goldenrod's flood!—
And ah, who can tell the pang I am knowing—
  The cry of lost April that leaps in my blood?

Old Men on Park Benches

It is a thing to break the heart upon,
Watching the old men gathering in the park
When Spring is on the earth bright with the sun,
Hearing their idle prattle from dawn till dark.
Whittling the hours away beneath blue skies
With clouds full-masted like a fleet of ships,
Always I see lost dreams burn in their eyes,
Hear echoes of lost songs upon their lips.
As robins watch them curiously and pass
From bough to bough, bright with a blossom's flame,
And the old men stare into the waking grass,
Youth must return, a dim-remembered name.
Shall I know too the word each daylight brings:
Life does not need them in its scheme of things?

Polo Player

Swift as an arrow in the wind he goes
Across the stretching velvet of the grass;
Like sudden music now he leaps and flows
In quickening rhythms as the hoofbeats pass.
They poise in space a fleeting moment, curve
Close to the ground again; now higher, higher,
They take the wind again; they leap, they swerve
With all the maddening passion of a fire.
The mallets whiz along the wind, they click
Staccato-like, again they whirr and rise;
Far quicker than the swiftest wind is quick
He sweeps across the field; his squinting eyes
Fast on the ball he sees it leap and roll . . .
His blood shouts in his veins, the goal, the goal!

Jungle

There is no sound except the closing of flowers
Burning with color underneath the brush,
And darkness falling on the leaves like showers
Promised, but never given. Night's blue hush
Is fast upon the jungle. Lilies stir,
As white as fallen stars, beside a stream
Turned suddenly to torrents of lavender
Along the jagged rocks. Half in a dream,
A cobra coils upon the emerald lace
Of scented fern; a tiger's amber eyes
Drowse in the fading light without a trace
Of fear, remembering day that bleeds and dies
By leaping to the Westward with a start
That brings the night's swift arrow to its heart.

The Captive

There is no turning back for him who goes
Down to the sea at seventeen or so;
The music of the sea that leaps and flows
In emerald tides will haunt him; he will go
Forever with the sunrise on his lips,
The purple dusk upon his brow, his ears
Throbbing with wings of gulls above the ships;
He will be a prisoner all his years.
Though full-blown moons may call, and he will yearn
For young breasts pale as lotus flowers are,
He must go on where darkening breakers turn
To silver fire beneath the Northern star.
Though he will beat on rocks eternally,
Forever he is captive of the sea.

Defeat in Springtime

When I had climbed upon the half-hidden boulder
I cocked my gun and laid it on my shoulder,
Waiting in silent ambush there until
My quarry came. Then I would shoot to kill.
The boughs above me quivered with emerald things:
A bud, a leaf, and scarlet blossomings
Bled on a twisted branch, blooms like a bell
That would not ring, but held me in their spell.
And patiently I waited with no sound
But the slow waking of the slumbering ground.
And suddenly, unheralded, it came,
A young buck far too beautiful for a name,
Brushing the shining boughs that spring had spread
Like a green heaven over his lifted head,
Creeping in measured rhythms, lyrical, slow,
As if it were a path he did not know,
And on the soft earth as his hooves were laid
It seemed that something of a poem were made.
Startled, he looked at me and I at him,
His eyes growing brighter, my eyes growing dim,
And for a breathless moment he cringed at bay,
His eyes saying more than any word could say.
And so I laid the gun beside my feet,
For spring was in the air and earth was sweet
With bud and leaf and tides of mountain laurel,
No time at all for life and death to quarrel.

Epitaphs

Her garden is the epitaph she writes
In living letters down her garden lane,—
Roses unfolding pink and yellow lights,
And crimson poppies steaming in the rain.
Madonna lilies are the songs she sings
In ivory notes pale as a half-blown moon;
Wistaria's fragrant bells the chimes she rings
When summer winds strike up a lavender tune.
Let other mortals venture, wrapping great
And shining deeds about them in far lands;
She is content within her garden gate,
Beneath her lilac boughs and flowering plum.
Shall not a thousand thousand Aprils come
When all their epitaphs are crumbled sands?

For an Old Sailor, Sleeping

How kind is night. Now you are not retired,
And four walls cannot hold you this dark hour.
Age falls like shackles from you; youth is fired
Into your veins again and all its power
Swings at a clipper's wheel battling the gale;
The wind is in your face, the sharp rain drips,
Turning to silver every tightening sail;
Now you are back again, one with the ships.
I shall blow out the candle, fold the book,
Marking it where you finished; I shall close
The door with one last brief and envious look,
Leaving you smiling where the North Star throws
Its light upon you as your dreams grow deep
With bright waves breaking on the shores of sleep.

Little I Dreamed

Little I dreamed when I was young and eager
  Watching the full moon plunging in the sky,
Breathing the breath of April's pale magnolias,
  Little I dreamed that loveliness could die.

And wading deep in fields of summer daisies,
  Watching them breaking, foaming at my knees,
My love upon my arm, my lips to hers,
  What could I know of death's dark silences?

Now as I see them swinging past my window,
  The youthful lovers with their eyes agleam,
Giving their hearts to beauty, drinking the starlight—
  How can I call to them and wake their dream?

The Moonflower

I can do less than pause above this flower
Bending a dark stem downward in the night,
Unfolding slowly, delicate and white,
Leaning upon the silence of the hour.
I could go far to-night, go very far,
Searching with weary footsteps and not find
Such beauty, unaware: a flower to blind
My eyes as though they feasted on a star.
Wrapped in the shadows and the quiet here,
Watching these quivering petals slowly stirred
From ivory slumber, needing no mortal's word
Telling the time to open crystal-clear,
Nor how and when to close its bloom again,
I ponder on the littleness of men.

Ship Model

Until he placed it on the mantel there,
The room was but a dingy place and only
Dark memories and ghosts of old despair
Would occupy his hours. Quiet and lonely
He sat and read a dusty volume through;
He drew his pension check and put away
His savings as old men are wont to do,
And count them over day by lengthening day.
But now there is new glamour in his eyes,
New conversation on his quivering lips,
As though he had returned from tropic skies
And brimmed with all the tales of seas and ships.
He sits and dreams to-night, and nods away—
And is his heart in Venice or Cathay?

Crystal Interlude

Can there be any peace beyond this hour,
Blue shadows lengthening as the daylight dies,
A book beneath a candle's lighted flower,
A cat with half-uncertain, emerald eyes,
Purring with contemplation on the floor,
The sharp wind lashing newly crystaled trees,
The measured swirl of snow against the door—
Can there be deeper, whiter silences?
The clock ticks onward to eternity,
Lightly as snow the minutes drift away;
Here is the heart's desire,—tranquillity
And dreaming at the closing of the day
Beside a fire that smolders spark on spark,
Throbbing like golden music in the dark.

I Saw Three Gulls

I saw three gulls along the morning sky,
 And listening, I heard white music beat
With each white wing as passionate as fire.
I watched them rising, swerving, climbing higher
 Above the dull procession of the street
Where steel and stone were mirrors for the eye.

What words were said before the day went by,
 What gold changed hands my lips could never tell;
I only know the diary of my heart
Can hold one thing to-night, set all apart,
 Ringing and chiming like a crystal bell:
I saw three gulls along the morning sky.

Summer Interval

Watching the slow stars light, we lay beneath
A dark magnolia where its branches spread
A hundred blossoms like moons above our head;
We listened, and we almost heard them breathe.

So pale they were, so delicately pale and white,
No word was said lest we should break the spell
Of shadows and of blossoms like a bell
Upturned to hold the quiet of the night.

Your hand in mine, the hours drifted away
Slower than fireflies through the summer air
Teaching us, dreaming beneath the shadows there
That silence speaks more than the lips can say.

Swamp Night

As quiet as words unspoken, daylight goes
Over the emerald water in bright escapes
And purple and blue as the ripening of grapes
The evening comes. As soft as a wing it flows
Over the trees, over the moss that drips
Like silent music from each gnarled limb,
And grasses heavy with dewfall shudder, dim,
Lost in the dark till their quivering tips
Are pointed with starlight. Paler than death
Swamp lilies open their petals apart
Until the beating of their wild heart
Ripples the water lighter than a breath.
Night slumbers on, forgetting at its gates
The sunrise like a golden shadow waits.

Old Soldiers' Home

The dim lamp flickers and the night grows late
As silence sweeps across the shadowed hill;
Only a late wind stirs the swinging gate
That creaks a fleeting moment, then is still.
The finger tips of moonlight touch the panes
Where frost has woven shimmering designs,
And starlight's sandals creep along the lanes,
Her garments brushing on the ivy vines.
Yet there is ever tumult in the heart
Of old, old soldiers dreaming in a bed;
Tumult that rings like silent bells, apart
From everything that they have heard or said.
Forever in their heart with each lost sun
Rings tumult of old battles lost or won.

Nostalgia

I must go South where honeysuckle holds
The gold of sunrise in each fluted bell,
Where dogwood on a twisted bough unfolds
More shining stars than any heart can tell.
I must go back where leagues of larkspur blow
As though the sky were tossing on a hill,
Where afternoons are long and winds are low
In quivering grasses till each blade is still.
I must go South where emerald water lies
Silent with opening lilies, mirroring
The burning beauty of the bright fireflies—
Where dusk falls blue and purple, ripening
Like berries toward the edges of the night,
And full moons rise like startled herons in flight.

Barren Lies the Land

Long since, these fields knew every April's thrust
Of thin new-bladed life that leapt like cries
Of victory from the winter's slumbering dust;
Once plowmen with old wisdom in their eyes,
As steadily as the day plows toward the night,
Went sweating down these fields. Once birds with wings
Of scarlet music shook plum branches white
With all the petaled glory that is Spring's.
Now barren lies the land. No new-turned rows
Lie throbbing with the passion of young rain;
No sunlight stirs red clover, no wind blows
The arrogant gold tassels of the grain.
Stars bloom and fall, days pass, and new moons climb,
But only silence ripens here, and Time.

Journey

The night came swift upon us. Like an arrow
The bow of darkness pointed to the road.
Blue shadows tangled at our feet; a sparrow
Was blinded by the darkness. Like a toad
It thumped against the branches and its wing
Was fettered with the nightfall. Its small eyes
Could single out no path for journeying;
No orphan star came wandering down the skies.
It quivered at our feet again, afraid.
As shadows grope, we picked our quiet way
Darker than death is dark, with nothing said.
The moon came up; the words we sought to say
Were lost in so much silver and the flight
Of one lone sparrow winging through the night.

Twilight in a Southern Town

The boxwood hedge grows blue with daylight's going
And down the silent street white lilacs lean
Upon the air. Magnolia trees are knowing
The rushing wings of sparrows swift and keen
To seek a quiet refuge through the night.
Deep-scented gardens mellowed in the sun
Stir with camellias in the drifting light
And ivory moonflowers open, one by one.
There is a splendor here that stills the blood
As soft winds ripple wistaria that falls
In deep cascades, a fragrant purple flood
Of beauty on old balconies and walls.
And at each gateway when the moon goes over,
The evening lingers like an ardent lover.

Old Woman Peddling Sunsets

I saw her on the city streets to-day
Crouched on the steps near some old corner-stone,
A tattered shawl around her; bent and gray
She seemed to hold a glory all her own.
And in her basket there, a hundredfold
Of gorgeous sunsets lighted up the place
Where car and cart went by as petaled gold
And crimson lent lost Aprils to her face.
Here was a flash of purple, here the pale
First yellow of the sunset, here the deep
Magenta petals, for a dime, on sale!—
Bright sunsets that a heart could hold, and keep!
How could I journey farther down the street
With dahlia blossoms at a woman's feet?

I Cannot Dance To-night

I cannot dance to-night for I have seen
A row of poplars dance against the sky,
Beheld them throwing tunics wild and green
Like graceful nymphs to winds that hurried by.
And in the gathered twilight of the day
My eyes have seen them quivering and tall,
Hold the new moon against their breast and sway,
Wrapped in the glory of a starlit shawl.
I cannot dance to-night, so let the rise
And fall of violins be soft, the clash
Of cymbals wake the night with melodies;
Let dancers sway and precious jewels flash.
I cannot dance to-night; I shall be still,
Remembering the poplars on a hill.

Charleston

You are an old, old lady by the sea,
With silver hair and cornflower-colored eyes,
A shawl of lavender wrapped carefully
About you. When the last gold daylight dies
And lilacs' breath is heavy on the air
Your fingers light bright candles one by one,
And sitting quietly beneath the flare
Of candle-light you see dark shadows run
Across the floor; you read a poem or two,
And drink the moonlight from your balcony
Turned into lace by shadows cold and blue.
You blow the candles out, and silently
You close your door and dream when night grows
    late,
Nor know there is a world beyond your gate.

Magnolia Gardens

I was a man before I entered here,
A man of flesh and blood and hair and bone,
But suddenly of all these I was none,
Nor was I earth nor sky nor wind nor air.
I was a tide of purple and a flare
Of crimson and a flood of yellow fire
Timeless and heedless, leaping higher and higher,
Chiming and surging like a passionate bell,
A sea of harmonies that rose and fell,
Gathering all sound and color in its swell;
Shadow and light crashing the shores of space,
Washing the centuries in a far thin line;
Here have I come on beauty face to face,
Here have I tasted beauty's lips on mine.

White Herons

Like frail white shadows now the herons pass
Along the darkening water's edge, nor stir
The water stretching like a mirrored glass
Where twilight falls in veils of lavender.

No feather quivers on each folded wing
That seeks a refuge where the willows fall
Upon the silent water, stenciling
Each leaf upon the lake. Serene and tall

The herons edge together. Breast to breast
And wing to wing, they watch the daylight go,
Nor stir beneath the quiet willows, pressed
As silently and white as drifted snow.

For a Poet's Bride

Spread sunlight on his toast, and spread it thickly,
And have it not too brown, and then upon it
Drop powdered violet petals lightly, quickly,
While mentally he works upon a sonnet.
For luncheon he must have delphinium broth,
Chilled water-lily salad and a rose,
Or give him Shasta daisy hearts, or both—
And bluebells will ring luncheon to a close.
Move quietly through the household. Never speak
Of pots and pans; talk only of the moon,
Of amber twilights and cool woods that reek
With fragrances of rain. Sing him a tune
And ask him softly with each fall of dew:
"One star dropped in your tea, my dear, or two?"

Lines for a Lad

This would I say to you,
O lad with eyes of blue
And hair of tangled gold,
And I would have you hold
This to your heart to-night;
These are the truest words
A man shall ever write.

These hours that you spend
With every flower your friend,
And music of a brook,
These are the holiest things
Of all rememberings
Within life's book;
There are no greater hours
For princes or for kings.

These dandelions you see
Like stars along the grass,
These butterflies that pass
In shining revelry—
These will endure,
So hold them close until the end;
They are your friend—
Of this alone you may be sure.

This would I say to you,
O lad with eyes of blue,

This would I say to you to keep,
And when the whole thing is over—
Laughter, grief, and lover,
All songs you sing, all tears you weep—
Dandelions by a brook
And yellow butterflies
Will still endure although your eyes
Are fast asleep;
Are fast asleep.

First Snowfall

This cedar was a cedar an hour ago,
As humble as the humblest roadside tree.
Now turning homeward in the violet glow
Of day's last light, I pass, and suddenly
It is a thing to feast the eyes upon.
So beautiful it is that I must kneel
Before this white cathedral pale as dawn;
I bow my head and quietly I feel
Its silent beauty flowing through my blood,
Its crystal arches reaching tier on tier;
Thank God that I must pass this patch of wood;
Thank God that I may kneel a moment here.

Words Before Twilight

Look long upon this daylight. Soon, too soon,
It will be utterly ravished by the moon.

Look long upon these sunlit leaves that blow
Like bells rung by the wind. Watch daylight go

As incense rises from a burning rose;
Drink deep the day's last amber, and bend close

To read blue grief in every pansy's face;
As darkness gathers watch a lizard trace

His glittering pathway to a hidden stone
Whose purple shelter he will seek alone.

Look long upon this daylight. Not again
Shall it return. A thousand thousand men

Can never bring it back though they may call
Until stars shatter and the mountains fall

And once again are dust. Look long upon
This day, for soon, too soon, it will be gone

As swiftly as a sparrow, as a breath—
As surely as no heartbeat follows death.

Last Encounter

How shall I die?—I who am passionate lover
Of all the tender little emerald things
Bursting upon a blackened bough to cover
A tree with sudden bloom; watcher of wings
Swift as an arrow down a Southern sky,
Comrade of fireflies burning in the dark,
Lover of new moons ripening, swinging high,
Of April lighting roses spark on spark;
Lover of ships and sails and thunderings
Of cold seas wild with foam;—How shall I die?
I shall die hard,—until my fists are black
Pounding upon Death's chest, tearing apart
His red eyes till he has me on my back
Wringing the blood's last rhythm from my heart!

The Sea

This wild and terrible beauty shall leave no pattern,
  No pattern upon the sand
When the last bright flash of jeweled foam is spended
  Like a coin within the hand.

This dark and emerald music lifting and roaring,
  Crashing, note upon note,
Shall leave no echo of its cold, clear singing
  For Time's deep throat.

Let us linger long and passionately on this shore
  Where the breakers fall,
Knowing there shall be left no fragment of its pattern,
  Knowing this is all.